THE JEWELS OF DARKNESS

THE JEWELS OF DARKNESS

MY SPIRITUAL JOURNEY

MARY ELIZABETH OCDS

ISBN: 978-1-965679-78-4 (sc)
ISBN: 978-1-965679-79-1 (e)

Rev. date: 02/05/2025

Dedication

To all those who have helped me on my spiritual journey - my thanks for all eternity.

In this revised edition I have added a few details which span my journey following the first publication in 2016. In 2022 I recorded the poems, prompted by a member of my Community who asked," What are you going to do for those who cannot see?" To my shame I had never given it a thought. The wonderful engineer, Matt,and David, who owned the professional studio(in the next village, would you believe it) enabled the recording. Fellow Carmelites, friends and I asked the Holy Spirit to help me speak them as they should be expressed. The result is beautiful. They come alive! The whole recording is soothing, loving and peaceful.

As a result some of the comments I made on the audio I have incorporated in this revised written edition.

There are no chapter headings, rather a series of sections which chart the progress of the spiritual insights(the Jewels), in groups of poems. A few within these sections have titles. Towards the end some 'poems' have more of my hand in them.

At the end of the book I say, 'And so my spiritual journey has led me through the darkness to the shores of the Kingdom of Love.' I then conclude my journey with a new poem. This links with the experience I had which resulted in the poem, ' I raise my hand and touch Your face.' (21/8/98).

This new poem is a 'wow'. It could not be more fitting. I am so grateful to have received it.

May this book bring you peace.

Mary Elizabeth OCDS. October 2024.

Foreword

This is a beautiful book. Like precious jewels these poems shine and sparkle and are a real 'sursum corda' to the spirit…a source of healing and inspiration to people of all classes on their journey through life. This is a book that soothes the mind, gives joy to the soul and enriches the spirit based as they are on Faith and Truth. A rich legacy that comes from an intimate blending of learning and life.

Father Ambrose McNamee, O.C.D.

'I will give you the treasures of darkness, riches stored in secret places, so that you may know that I am the Lord, the God of Israel, who summons you by name.'

Isaiah 45 v3.
Given to me by a nun who had read the original book.

The Introduction

I write this introduction in Lourdes, this great place of love and healing, where the presence of Our Lady and Our Lord is tangible in the atmosphere, the Masses, the prayers and in the pilgrims whose love and compassion for one another reveals Jesus and His Beloved Mother working amongst us.

Over 30 years ago I was searching for God, for a deeper experience and while the beauty of the life of consecration and spiritual union was revealed so was the path to this. I was horrified. I was confronted with the way of the Cross. This was a mystical experience and one of which I was very afraid. But naturally, when the Light of God shines on the soul our spiritual darkness -which needs transformation- is revealed. With God's grace comes responsibility for this spiritual help. We either respond or we do not. God is, however, very patient with our slowness to respond - and merciful to our faults.

The journey I undertook was both beautiful and, at times, very painful. Yet it was through the suffering (and cleansing) that some of the beauty was revealed. It wasn't all pain though!!

These reflections came before, after prayer or independently. I just had to write. Though they were of help to me they seem to have universal application to those on the spiritual path. These beautiful jewels of insight into God, Our Lady and Our Lord came through my darkness and ignorance.

I hope they comfort and strengthen you.

The Call and the Challenge

March 1983. Passion Sunday. Retreat day.

I desire nothing except to be in the way of God
In the way of His finding
And in the way of His seeking,
My being poured out in the power of His overcoming.
I do not understand this desire,
Mysterious in its beckoning,
Issuing from the deepest core
With an energy of call beyond all fathoms
And an awareness of Life beyond all my living
But this I do know - it comes from God.

It is a longing for consummation
Of self giving at the highest, deepest, broadest level,
Of the utmost sanctity and beauty,
It bespeaks of holiness And the radiance of purity.
It tells of death in the most creative sense
That life may issue forth for the freeing and healing of
souls,
And the joy be that of the battle won.
The morning section: then later in the day -

And now I see and I am afraid,
Afraid of the pain, and the rejection,
The misunderstandings, of the way itself now revealed.
This depth I did not choose, nor perceive.
My spirit shrinks, my heart faints, I enter dread
And rank fear. I wish to run, far, far into the night,
The sweat pouring from my soul, knowing
That this _is_ the way
And that there is no other
No relief, no haven of endless comfort and freedom from
pain
But only the endless going-on, in the midst of pain,
And learning to die.

O God, what a death I have to die
What pain I have to bear, what night of darkness
And depth of purification. I cannot. Nor can I retreat,
Save into torment and self-centred stultification.
I am so weak, this path is narrow and hard, always hard.

And you say, "This is the way I trod. Bear it,
There is no other. And when you come, to place those
first hesitant steps on the ground,
Know that this must be for you
And those who would follow Me.
The self must die in order to be born again
And so be raised by the Spirit to give of itself in love,
For such _is_ the way of overcoming."

Battling On!!

The life breath is squeezed out of my soul.
Parched, the dry river bed lies arid and desolate.
Nothing moves.
Clouds come, then go, all is silent
And the ground bakes in the heat, drier and drier.
I call and my cry comes back
Sharp and clear in the empty space.....
And yet I am held, I am not alone,
Some strange sense of Being
Undergirds this desert within me.
I crawl into the shadow of the rock
To rest or die, no water comes.
"Why?" I ask, and "How long? each soul must be fed."
But nothing comes
Nothing, only time and that constant present Absence.

20/2/92

Aridity

Then in 1997, the first jewel of Our Lady, followed by the first jewels of God in 1998 and 2001.

O loving mother
Ever watchful and still
Bless our Order with peace
That we may behold Our Lord
In faith and joy made flesh
In wills assenting through grace
The Word of God manifest.

O loving mother
Hear our prayer, intercede for us
Strengthen us to bear the sword's pierce of our hearts
That we may stand alongside you
As you love your Son and share His pain
Ever faithful and true.

O gracious mother
Teach us by your life, your trust
To let Our Lord lead and guide
Each day, each moment, whatever befall
That we may follow too
The path of self giving love
And gentle surrender.

Solemnity of Our Lady of Mount Carmel
16/7/97

Is silence, silence of the heart,
The sanctuary of the soul
The place of victory?
The place where the overcoming
Of all that is not of God, by Christ within
Is the stillness, the peace, the quiet after the storm?

Is prayer then the journey, the shedding
Of thoughts and desires, the loosing
Of the soul's tackiness with the world, the flesh and
the devil?
Spiralling downwards, inwards to Christ crucified,
awaiting my sin,
My separation from God, thirsting to hold my
waywardness
To loving, tired arms of reconciliation?

And is that meeting the place where
The silence begins, deepens to receive more,
More of the world's needs, until all is silence
And my tiny soul stares, awestruck,
At the heart of God, where all is silence
Redeeming, glorified silence
The silence of union?

20/3/98

I raise my hand and touch Your face
I caress the air and rejoice in Your beauty
O God, my God, eternal Love and grace.

Beneath the vision of sense
The eye of the Spirit gazes in awe
Upon Your Being, of utter delight
And such sweet tenderness of Loving.

I am enraptured by Your Beauty
Revealed in darkness, without sound, only Presence
Depth upon depth of God, exquisite to behold
And majesty beyond all other.
O God, my God, how beautiful You are.

I drink deep draughts of Beauty
I adorn myself with the jewels of Love
All in darkness, without sound, without sight.
I possess nothing yet I have been given
All I could have longed for
As I gaze, O God, upon the beauty of Your Face
The radiance of Your Being,
In the darkness, such utter darkness,
And adore.

21/8/98

Father, You are before me
And Your being surrounds me
So quiet, so gentle, like the first flakes of snow
Falling softly, softly to the ground.
But You do not invade me
You are apart, waiting for me to open
The door of my heart.
And you are so patient with all my shortcomings.
Each moment you are as now.
O that I could respond to You
And lovingly greet You in this constant presence
And adore You, God, for ever
The beginning and the end
Of all our living.
Amen.

17/12/01

Then Jesus and Our Lady came, showering jewels of Light and Beauty amid the suffering that enveloped both. 2003-2015.

You came so softly, so gently,
And lived among us, for us.
You gave every atom of your being
To lift up our distress and abandonment of our Father.
Yet we turned away, left you comfortless.

You carried on, so bravely, so lovingly,
Bearing our pain, our ignorance,
Embracing our darkness,
Confronting our accuser in death and beyond death
Bringing light and peace to waiting souls.

You are present now, so still, so quiet
Holding us in our blindness
Seeking our loving assent to all that this moment may bring
That, open in our soul's depths, you will wrap us in Light,
To become atoms of Your glorified Body.

10/12/03

'He will live with them and they shall be his people'

And so I gazed upon Your Face
My soul seeing nothing but darkness
Yet Your gaze met mine
And I beheld Love
And Love entered my soul.
I became my true self before you.
Such Beauty, such Friendship
Your own true self before me in that gaze
Of wordless beholding,
I, in awe and wonder
You, in loving mercy and fidelity.
Silence.

You went
And I longed for You to return
This magnificent Saviour
My truest friend.
I realised that I had to go on in faith
Beholding You in the darkness, yet hidden,
Waiting for Your gaze to meet mine again
But always beholding
Never to look elsewhere

7/3/05.

Stillness, absolute stillness,
My soul before You, facing You,
Moment in, moment out,
No change from this gaze,
The vision beheld in darkness
And in the discipline of obedience -
That training of the eyes of the soul to look
Neither to the right nor the left, only ahead -
To see through the window of this moment
You, hidden but present, and, in this beholding,
To hold before Your perspective the activity of this
moment,
Learning to trust in Your direction through
The flux of events, energies, emotions, decisions,
Seeing eternity beholding time with
Wisdom, compassion, love.

Beloved Lord, the journey of living is this,
To sharpen our gaze through this darkness
And through seeing nothing, feeling nothing
To be taught by You to rest in stillness
And let faith illuminate this darkness
And apparent absence.

17/4/08 'In darkness and secure' St John of the Cross

Those beautiful eyes gaze upon me
And Love radiates from Your face
Like rays from the sun
And my soul relaxes.

How can the world be so indifferent!
How can mankind not see the tenderness that enfolds us
And longs to love us into God's own being
Brushing away the darkness to bestow Light
Sparkling like crystal into each heart.

The Love that searches, never gives up
Waits patiently at the door of each moment
For a welcome
But frequently is ignored, shut out, spat upon
Or tortured.

And those beautiful eyes gaze with Love
Through the pain and offer Life
In exchange for death.

My most beautiful Lord.

25/4/05

Suddenly I realised her beauty,
Shimmering like an exquisite jewel
Radiant, outpassing all other souls,
Our Mother, the joy of Carmel.

In a second I saw what purity meant,
Transfixed in awe my heart melted
At the love which enfolded her,
Issued from her and embraced us all
And held us to the darling heart of God.

In that embrace the soul is free
Free to love and adore
Free to grow and become strong,
Held, loved, nurtured in Our Mother's arms
To gaze enraptured in spirit
Upon that Word which she heard
And allowed entrance to her soul
And so to all of us.

Amen. So let it be, dearest Mother.

14/8/05
Transferred Solemnity of the Assumption

The sacred centre of Mary,
The gift of God to her, she returned in love.
There is no greater beauty
For it is the image of God in her,
This place of glorious self-giving, communion of spirit,
And dynamic of chastity,
The essence of the soul
Which clothes the flesh in the majesty of union
The wedding of spirit to spirit
The Holy Spirit to the created spirit
In which He asks to dwell
And incarnate the Word so that He may speak
Through her to all mankind.

Take us, dear Mother, into that sacred place
Lead us and guide us through your perfection
To Christ our Lord
Mindful that the journey entails the Heaven
Owned through the Passion, where true self-giving
Learns the joy of the Word spoken in victory
For us all.

14/8/05 Transferred Solemnity of the Assumption

What must it be, this light, this radiance?
To be before the Father, Your Son,
Held in His Holy Spirit?
To know your Father's supreme Love
Blessing your soul - and for eternity?
To be received into the sanctuary of the Most High?
Journeying from Maid to Queen
From bearing the Word incarnate to
Rising in the Word glorified?
No words. Wonder and joy
A union of love which welcomes all mankind,
Your royalty the beauty of the soul that said "Yes"
For all time,
For whom the sword became the sceptre
The symbol of the reign of love.

14/8/05 Transferred Solemnity of the Assumption The
Queenship of Mary, the courts of Heaven

I glimpsed the beauty of the soul
Shimmering in light, almost golden,
Of a purity of being unknown
In this world of matter.
This beauty is a dignity of transcendence,
But of the creation of Love,
Where the loving arms of our Father
Embrace it forever
And hold it to Himself for union.
Such is our journey,
Borne in the heart of our Beloved Lord
Through all sorrow and struggle
To discover this inheritance,
And in this vision of deep joy
Know and be known -
And rest in such fulfilment
That our life is adoration
And the wonder of belonging.

1/5/07

In the foreshadowing of our destiny
This jewel of God's delight
Touched earth in the arms of loving souls.
Her soul was held in union
Growing into that maturity of being
Wherein Gabriel would speak
And she would hear
Within the astonishment of true humility
And a willing obedience born of faith.

This mighty God, whose loving mind none can fathom
Bestowed His purity upon her
So she was untouched by sin
But bore the suffering of it -
In depths that make us shudder.
For she carried her Son in body, soul and spirit,
While He loved her and taught her
As Her Master and Lord
This way of prayer and service and atonement,
This jewel of God's delight - and ours.

10/9/07

This nightmare was no fantasy
Created from paranoid intuition.
Your dread was issuing from Truth
And the depths of pain to be entered
And borne for us
Beyond human conception.

You knew more terror in that Garden
Than most of us together will ever feel.
And you began your crucifixion there
Bleeding in soul and spirit
Your body conveying the horror to come
In sweat turned to blood,
The beginning of this aweful sacrifice.

And, as now, Your companions slept
Oblivious of Your agony's real purpose.
They did not see the Word
Subsuming the purpose of the Incarnation,
Our redemption,
And emptied of Your glory.

In loving obedience to Your Father
Maybe neither did You,
Save that this was to be Your path,
The terrible will of Him who sent You.
And
That there would be no ram
Tangled in the thicket to spare Your death.

Behold this Man given for us -
And worship this King of all kings,
Of a Majesty and grandeur
No human can absorb
Save in the heart's adoration.

Gethsemane.

Did the sword pierce your heart, dear Mother
When you heard of his arrest?
This mystical sword of Love
Intertwined in a union of suffering.
And did you ache with that dread that overcame Him,
So close you were - and are?

You were so brave
From the moment of Gabriel's message,
In what could have been humiliation and social rejection,
To the scandal of the Crucifixion.
Such courage, lending strength to your beloved Jesus
Through all your heart's energy,
Of such purity that it could comfort your Lord.

7/3/08

Were you waiting by her bedside,
Watching, loving her as she had watched You
Dying on the Cross?
Maybe Your presence was unseen
But surely she would have known
Your two hearts intertwined
From beginning to end.

Did You then hold her body in Your arms
As she held You, taken down from the Cross,
But, this time, there was no sorrow, only joy
For the Lord of Glory had embraced you
And took you to Himself,
Transforming you into your risen state
While carrying you through creation and Paradise
Until you came to Heaven
And gazed upon Our Father,
The Spirit revealing the majesty and splendour
Shared with His Son.

You saw now the necessity of His plan,
Why God chose you to bear His Son
And why sorrow beset you amid the joy.
It all became clear.
Now you are transfigured in the Glory,
Lost in wonder and praise.

The angels surround you.
Love envelops you.

Our Lord has brought you home.
O what beauty, what inexpressible joy.

Pray for us, Mother of God,
That we too may enter the joy of Heaven.

Solemnity of the Assumption 2011

It was not just the physical torture
But the unseen attacks - spiritual, psychic,
Emotional, intellectual.
That no one has portrayed, except
The horrific effects on His face
From which the soul gazes outwards.

It is the realms of all these
Existing throughout creation that He bore
And redeemed in matter, space and time,
Every atom and particle.
All the disharmony surrounded with transfiguring Love
In acceptance of the evil, the darkness,
And the magnificent pursuit of loving it away,
The energy restored to Light and Truth.

He cleansed and purified everything
Even death, dying and Hell.
There is nothing He has not embraced
And healed.
"It is finished." The victory is won.
But it is not fulfilled as yet
For He has to die and rise in each soul
To bring the work to completion,
The reunion of all with the Father.
His offer is present, always present.
But will we respond? Or turn away?
Might there be a time limit on His mercy?

6/4/12: Good Friday

Love filled her, grew from her,
Surrounded her like a cloak
As she gazed upon Him,
The fulfillment of her 'Yes'.
This tiny form, snug in His swaddling clothes,
Lying on the hay,
This bed of fodder which He would become in Himself
To feed mankind.
She saw only this baby
Evidence of the Spirit's conception
Bringing amazement, joy, adoration
As should all actions of grace in the soul.

And did those tiny eyes gaze upon her
In a sense of blessing and thanksgiving?

21/12/14

Set me as a seal upon Your heart
That I may walk enclosed
As in a garden
Fragrant and lovely
Restful and still,
Where I may hear the silence
Coming as a rain of gentle drops
Or as a whisper, soothing
And strengthening.

Who can describe the seal of Love?
It is there by your gift
And, once engraved, a distinct mark
Of ownership, of covenant,
The sacrament of Love -
Where the communion can be endless
In the heart betrothed.

2015

We are held in Your heart
The whole of the universe is there embraced
The natural world, human kind,
Every grain of sand on the seashore
The myriad of stars and farthest space,
The spiritual realm, known and intuited though unseen.
Love and mercy are the core,
In unfathomable depths
Where the echoes are always
"Come to Me and rest,
Let peace fill your soul,
Let Me remake you in My Image
For then you will shine with the light of My glory,
But - share my sorrow, my pain
For all those who disregard Me
Who reject My commandments
And deepen the sin of this world.
Bear with Me these souls
And carry them into My Mercy.

12/4/15 Divine Mercy Sunday

And while Jesus and Our Lady revealed such beauty they taught me how to find Light and Growth through my temptations, suffering and pain. 2002 - 2009.

I became aware of Your tenderness
Your gentle presence, in the silence.
Such loving patience and mercy.
And I longed to be with you
To love You and rest. Rest from the struggle,
The battering of my mind, my desires,
From constant temptation and dog-gone human frailty.
"Persevere," You say: "all will be well
For I have conquered all through Love
And that is what you must do.
Love, not fight,
Surround the temptation with offering to My Love,
Which overcomes all evil.
Let go of the problem into My hands,
And watch and wait while I work to change for good."

17/10/02

"Embrace the pain", You say, "welcome it."
What is it but that you do not want?
It is only doing its duty.
In its own way it is a servant.
A warning - of danger, of illness,
Of unhealed memories and the need for forgiveness,
To the abuser, to one's own self, for weakness, for sin
Of the separation from one another
And from God
The cosmic disorder
The spiritual conflict
Pain is a friend in disguise
Meet it with blessing.
Try that."

26/3/03

How can it be that You draw me
Deeper and deeper into the fire
Though I feel no flame?
That You ask me to come as your bride
And live in union with You?
I, the unclean, the sinful, taken
Taken so lovingly into Your heart,
The wedding held there
And the ceremony beheld by Heaven
And Our Mother.
This bridal gown is Your gift,
The purity of being which is Your image
Released in my soul, nurtured slowly
Into the redemption of Your grace
Where with open arms You beckon me home
And tell me You love me.
Is this the rest I have journeyed to?
Where I am at peace?
The silence of Your Love draws me,
I long to stay there, still, so still
In this union of no sound
But loving Presence.
And draw to Your heart those souls
Who know You not, or hurt and ache
With the pain of living,
For You to bathe them with Your blessing
And free them, like me, to journey into

The depths of joy and the wonder of You.
O help me to be faithful. I so want to be.
Amen.

1/9/05

Hidden within Your Life - I live.
I do not <u>live</u> elsewhere
There I die or am depleted.
Held within Your Body and Your Blood
I flower into union
And see that there is no other way.
There I am baptised in the Spirit,
Immersed in the sacrifice of Love,
Offer my body, my life, into the pain
Bleeding with You the wounds of sin,
Ignorance and folly,
Bearing them with You and for You
As You have taught me,
"Father, forgive them, they know not what they do."
And so I take the pain, the disharmony, as best I can.
I take it from them on their behalf
And bring it into Your Body and Blood,
To be redeemed and transformed.
And in the bearing I discover joy.
<u>There</u> is Your assent to the offering,
The prayer is heard
And peace comes.
And so the work begins again
And must continue to the End
Until all is reconciled and made whole.
For such is Love.
Amen.

23/8/06

I look back and wonder
Wonder at the love and faithfulness
That embraced my path
And held me to You through all my scrapes, falls and doubts.
Now I see that I had to retrace my life,
Guided by Your loving care,
To that point where the wound was inflicted
Terrible in accuracy, deadly in intent
And reclaim the poisoned flesh, soul, spirit
In all its clothing.
Drinking the chalice so offered,
Discovering through this bizarre and disturbing journey
The transformation that lay hidden in the empty cup.
And so I am now reborn
Born again to live as I should from those early days,
With a soul that is mine, a spirit that is free,
A sense of selfhood completed.
I am astonished but with an overwhelming thankfulness.
I have been watched over by You and Our Lady,
Your Holy Spirit guiding with tenacity and dedication.
Thank You Father, dear Father, for You
Your Son, Your Holy Spirit.
Thank You again and again and again
For all eternity.
Amen.

17/3/09

I entered that sanctuary
That holy place of rest
Where all sin and suffering has been overcome
And I knew peace and rest of soul.
In this eternal silence
I understood the victory won for us
And here I brought the souls of those I hurt
And undid the pain.
I held the hurt I caused, I felt it, I owned it,
Seeking through grace that release and healing for them
Only His redemption could fulfil.

And here I saw the wonder of Him,
His Love, so misunderstood,
And the divinity revealed in His humanity.

And I tiptoed in awe at the transcendence of God
And the reality of Him.

1/4/09

Lourdes

My first visit 2007 and my last 2015. I received deep healing of spirit in 2007. My love of Our Lady deepened even more during these visits (2007-10, 2012-15). Our Lord was very active too!!

So many wheelchairs
So many longing for help
Disfigurement of body
Crippling disease
Stretchered
But all loved and cherished
In this place of comfort,
Following in the procession behind the Virgin
Or Our Lord in the Blessed Sacrament
Seemingly endless numbers
Of the sick, the hurt and wounded,
In spirit, mind and body.

As though the world came today.

This love, this longing,
The prayer rising, rising until lost
In the mystery of God,
Borne in the suffering of Christ
And His beautiful Mother -
For she felt the sword pierce her heart
And knew the pain of grief
And human tragedy.

And then they come,
To encircle the Grotto
That place of vision and intercession.
Did I see the rock face worn smooth
By hands pleading and hearts breaking -
Or love for this woman who mothers us all?

Then the candles, bent, listing sideways,
Drooping, though tall at first,
The many stands
The many prayers
The love
The desperation
"Holy Mother of God, pray for us,"
"Our Lady of Lourdes, pray for us"
And, "St. Bernadette, pray for us,"
For you first saw her,
Saw her in her loveliness
And heard her desire to save us,
By carrying us to her Son -
In whose heart she rests
And He at one with hers.

Everywhere - healing,
Cleansing of the soul
Redemption and transformation.
Thousands of rosary prayers,
Adoration of Our Lord,
His presence in the Eucharist,
The loving anointing of the sick,
The water of the baths -
A sacred offering .... so sacred ....

And then
Places of prayer
Magnificent buildings and art
Priests, monks and nuns,
The world's nations and races
Stories of healing
But above all - loving care -
And unity in the Spirit -
All from the visit of the Mother of God
To a poor "peasant" girl
Who lovingly obeyed this "Beautiful Lady"
And shocked mankind into belief.

16/6/07 Solemnity of the Sacred Heart, Lourdes

I see now the privilege
Encapsulated in the pain.
From the blessing at the first
There was the humiliation
And then the deep sword thrust
Of warning at the dedication.
You were indeed without sin
You could not have borne such agony
For the most pure sinner would have died
And it was the purity of your love
That joined with your humility
Gave you the strength to endure.
Yes, you were mother to a beautiful son
But there was the Deity
And that aweful union with holiness
Wherein was the vocation and the pain
Not for sadistic misery
But the most generous offering
For the work of salvation
Your hearts at one
Your spirit held in His, Your hidden Lord
And wonderful Saviour.

You were chosen to bring Life
Created for this magnificent service
Of largely silent witness
But in your silence we heard
The Word made flesh
And manifest among us

And a fidelity of love to Him
That no one can gainsay.

Pray for us Mother of God
Pray for our fidelity
That we may be your true children
And love your Son.

Lourdes 20/6/10

Beautiful, holy Mother
You love us so much.
You bore such pain and distress
With Jesus and for Him.
You know suffering so well.
I see how you long that your children
Turn aside from sin, find your help
In sickness of soul and body.
We come to you, to rest in your Immaculate Heart
And draw comfort.
We know that you will intercede for us
And that we will receive from your Son
Some answer that He feels best.

How often you have appeared to encourage,
Warn, teach us - or just spoken to guide.
Dear Mother, help us to stay with you,
Day by day in our hearts,
That with you we may be with Jesus,
Loving and serving.
Amen

12/9/13 Lourdes

Is this the miracle of Lourdes
This sharing of our pain
And the love that Our Mother bestows
Upon the aching heart,
She who shared His crucifixion in spirit?
And the ministry of Our Beloved Lord
In sacrament and inner blessing,
Lifting, lifting some - maybe all - of the pain?

And then the prayer -
The thanksgiving for help, restoration to life,
Of lives transformed through the intercession
Of Mary to her Son.
And so the awareness of consecration to the path
Of faith, obedience and truth
Of sharing the burden of suffering for others
And being with Our Lady at the foot of the Cross
But also in the joy of the Resurrection.

Is this the miracle of Lourdes?

Immaculate Heart of Mary, 16/6/07

Being Naughty!!

'Love bade me welcome'
But I was messing around.
Love said, "Sit and eat"
But I said, "Thank you, in a minute."
The minute became an hour
Then two hours - and more.
Love did <u>not</u> say
"Why are you wasting my time?"
Nor, "You stood me up, we had a date."
But "I love you, please come, I am waiting,"
And still I delayed -
"I have so much to do Lord."

Then, Love wept, and I, smitten with shame,
Hung my head and cried.
I looked at the One who gave me all my being,
Whose faithfulness pursued my neglect,
And came and sat.
I ate repentance for my folly
And distance for my delay
Yet mercy came to meet me, forgiveness clothed me,
And love 'bade me welcome' once more.

I said, "<u>Please</u> help me not to do this again."
Love said, "It is in your nature, you minx,
You don't half give me grief
But I still love you and wait for you."
I looked at Him.
This <u>is</u> true love, I thought,

Real endurance. I was full of admiration.
And I bound myself to remain,
In all my weakness,
To sit and be with my most intimate friend,
My brother, my lover, my husband,
My Master and my Lord,

And this time, I ate - joy and peace
And a stillness of Loving.

With thanks to Rev. George Herbert. His beautiful poem,
'Love bade me welcome.' 24/9/07

Reflections on our secular world.

My little soul peeped out at the stars,
The heavens, mysterious space,
Galaxy upon galaxy, beautiful planets.
I thought of those who said,
"We have found no God here,
The only essence is protons, neutrons, atoms,
Black holes, light years......"
And saw their confusion might resolve
In the inner exploration,
The galaxies of the Spirit
The light years of silence
An endless journey of meeting,
Encounter with Truth and Being,
The dimensions that should order this world.

18/4/08

Walking to church Rosary intoning
The little Asda van passed by.
'Where are you going,' I thought,
'Jesus is dying on the Cross.
Have you not heard that
He is the Saviour of the world?
We should all be on our knees
In thanksgiving, adoration and worship?'

The van disappeared from sight
A symbol of secularisation
And yet again Jesus is ignored
Left outside hearts, souls, minds.

The van was sweet, like a 'Dinky' toy,
No harm nor insult intended,
Just going about the necessary work
Of our supermarket world.
But I longed that it would stop
And "doff its cap" to Our Lord
If only for a second.

Good Friday 22/4/11 written 24/4/11

Transformation.

What was once desert, barren and arid
Is now fertile, bedecked with flowers.
The rocks are the same
The area is unchanged
Yet it is beautiful - and such peace!
There is a strange transformation of this familiar place,
Rays of golden light glisten on those sharp edges
And what once hurt is smooth
Even that howling, cruel wind
Is now a soft breeze.
The glory of the Lord is here.

Is this the gospel that we must proclaim?
The Presence that we must pray into all those desert
wildernesses
Of the human soul and spirit?
The transfiguration of pain into God?

10/12/13

God has the final word

You cannot capture Heaven
It has to be revealed
In a flower, a colour, the song of a bird,
In shape and texture, in perfume,
In a person.
It is elusive because hidden in mystery
Yet known in Love and wonder,
The substance of Spirit incarnated,
But also beyond this visible life
And known to those who gaze in rapture
Upon the Beloved.
For there it is all that there is
And ever shall be.
Amen.

11/5/06

'And so my spiritual journey has led me , through the darkness, to the shores of the Kingdom of Love.'

'The Lord showed me the holy city which had the glory
of God, and it shone like a precious stone.'
Antiphon, Vespers of St. Teresa of Avila.

I saw this exquisite jewel
The beauty beyond expression
So clear, reflecting Light
And drawing me
Drawing me onwards to find
Complete union of soul and spirit,
Mysterious yet radiating
Wonder, Presence and Love.
It was the Holy City
Sparkling in the darkness of my soul,
The Jewel of all jewels,
The home of God,
Father, Son and Holy Spirit.

19/10/24

'The Lord bless you and keep you,
The Lord make his face to shine upon you,
And give you peace.'

Remember, you are loved,
Always loved.

About the Author

Mary Elizabeth loves Classical music. Favourite composers are JS Bach, Rachmaninov, Chopin, Vaughan Williams and many more. She loves Classical ballet- Swan Lake, Sleeping Beauty. In opera she loves Tosca, La Traviata among others. For Choral music the St John Passion, Handel's Messiah. In the garden she loves old varieties of roses for their exquisite perfume. If age had not caught up with her she would play tennis but she loves walks in the country and bird watching. She loves donkeys, cats and dogs.

She is a Roman Catholic and a lay member of the Teresian Carmelite order. She looks forward to Heaven when the time comes and meanwhile gets on with the living and loving that is the vocation of every Christian. When she fails she asks Our Lord for forgiveness and He helps her continue this journey. He is very patient!!

The proceeds of these jewels will go to the Order of Carmelites Discalced with my love and thanksgiving.

www.ingramcontent.com/pod-product-compliance
Lightning Source LLC
Chambersburg PA
CBHW061712120626
46550CB00003B/1194